Arlington

MW01146802

A Guide to Arlington House,
The Robert E. Lee Memorial
Virginia

Produced by the
Division of Publications
National Park Service

U.S. Department of the Interior
Washington, D.C. 1985

Using This Handbook
Arlington House, The Robert E. Lee Memorial sits
on a bluff in northern Virginia overlooking Arlington
Cemetery, the Potomac River, and the City of
Washington. This handbook is published in support
of the National Park Service's management policies
and interpretive programs at the park. Part 1 of the
handbook introduces the reader to General Lee and
the site. Park 2 presents a brief historical account of
the house and its occupants, the Custises and the
Lees. Part 3 provides concise information on the
house and grounds.

National Park Handbooks, compact introductions to
the great natural and historic places administered by
the National Park Service, are designed to promote
understanding and enjoyment of the parks. Each is
intended to be informative reading and a useful
guide before, during, and after a park visit. More
than 100 titles are in print. This is Handbook 133.

Library of Congress Cataloging in Publication Data
Main entry under title:
Arlington House, the Robert E. Lee Memorial.
(National park handbook; 133)
Supt. of Docs. no.: I29.9/5:133
1. Arlington House (Va.)—Guide-books. 2. Lee,
Robert E. (Robert Edward), 1807-1870—Homes—
Virginia—Arlington County. 3. Custis family. 4. Lee
family. I. United States. National Park Service.
Division of Publications. II. Series: Handbook
(United States. National Park Service. Division of
Publications); 133.
F234.A7A75 1985   975.5'295   85-18925
ISBN 0-912627-23-9

Contents

Part 1

Welcome to Arlington House

Honoring a Great Leader

Confederate Gen. Robert E. Lee, youngest son of Revolutionary War hero Henry "Light Horse Harry" Lee, was born January 19, 1807, at Stratford Hall, a Lee estate in Westmoreland County, Virginia. Lee graduated second in his West Point class of 1829 and two years later married Mary Anna Randolph Custis, one of Martha Washington's great-granddaughters.

Pages 4-5: Arlington House, The Robert E. Lee Memorial.

Pages 10-11: Arlington Memorial Bridge, seen from the east portico of Arlington House, links the mansion with Lincoln Memorial.

Robert E. Lee, born of two distinguished Virginia families, was raised to follow the path of honor and duty. A devoted son, an outstanding West Point cadet, and a United States Army officer for 32 years, Lee came face to face in 1861 with a most difficult choice: Allegiance to the American nation and the flag he had served so long and well, or loyalty to his native Virginia.

A lieutenant colonel in the cavalry on the Texas frontier, Lee was ordered back to Washington in 1861 when Texas seceded from the Union. Through the long and tedious months of his Texas tour, he had hoped some way would be found to avert civil war. On his return to Arlington, the estate bequeathed to his wife Mary by her father, George Washington Parke Custis, Lee was offered the command of a large Union army being organized to take the field against the South. He courteously declined the offer, expressing his opposition to both secession and war and an unwillingness to participate in an invasion of the Southern states. The next day news of Virginia's adoption of the Act of Secession reached Lee. Not wishing to be placed under orders he could not follow, Lee wrote his resignation from the U.S. Army on April 20, 1861.

Two days later, Lee bid farewell to his wife and children and to Arlington and boarded a train to Richmond to take command of Virginia's military forces. Well aware that Arlington's commanding site high on a bluff overlooking the Nation's Capital would make it an early target of federal capture, Lee may have wondered if he would ever return to the house and estate he had known since childhood.

As the war progressed, Arlington House was occupied by the Union Army. The Lees lost title to the house in 1864 when Arlington was seized for non-payment of taxes and acquired by the Federal Government for $26,800.

In 1873 George Washington Custis Lee, the Lees' eldest son, sued the Federal Government for the return of the property charging that the seizure had been illegal. The U.S. Supreme Court agreed and restored the estate title to Lee in 1882. By then, however, several thousand war dead had been buried in Arlington's hills, and Custis Lee accepted $150,000 from the U.S. Government for the property. Union fortifications built on the property during the Civil War were absorbed by Fort Myer, by Arlington National Cemetery, and subsequently by the Department of Agriculture. Freedman's Village, a settlement established in wartime for emancipated slaves, operated there for about 20 years. At one time it provided homes and jobs for 2,000 residents and contained three churches, a school, an orphans home, and a home for the aged. From 1900 to 1933 the Department of Agriculture operated a 330-acre experimental farm on estate land near the Potomac River.

With the passage of time, many people came to appreciate Robert E. Lee's role in reuniting the American nation after the Civil War. The Confederate general's example inspired men and women of his day to lay down old grievances and get on with the job of rebuilding a new and better America. Lee used his influence to move away from the bitterness of war to reunion and peace. "Madam," Lee admonished a Southern visitor in his last years, "don't bring up your sons to detest the United States Government. Recollect that we form one country now. Abandon all these local animosities and make your sons Americans."

U.S. Rep. Louis Cramton of Michigan learned of Lee's greatness from his father, a Union soldier who served in Virginia for nearly the entire war. In 1925 Congress unanimously passed Cramton's legislation establishing the Lee Mansion National Memorial. In testimony supporting his bill, Cramton declared: "I believe it is unprecedented in history for a nation to have gone through as great a struggle as that was, and in the lifetime of men then living to see the country so absolutely reunited as is our country . . . there was no man in the South who did more by his precept and example to help bring about that condition than did Robert E. Lee."

Restoration of Arlington House was begun in 1925 by the War Department and has been continued by the National Park Service since 1933. Today Arlington House serves as a stately memorial to Robert E. Lee, welcoming guests daily from around the nation and the world. Across the Potomac River stands the Lincoln Memorial commemorating the President who gave his life to preserve the Union. Thus Arlington Memorial Bridge, which links the two memorials, symbolizes the reconciliation these two leaders sought between the North and the South.

1807   Robert Edward Lee is born on January 19 at Stratford Hall in Westmoreland County, Virginia, the fifth child of Henry "Light Horse Harry" Lee and his second wife, Ann Hill Carter.

1811   Robert and his family move to Alexandria.

1818   His father dies and Robert takes on family responsibilities.

1829   Lee graduates second in his West Point class. He is posted as an army engineer to Cockspur Island near Savannah, Georgia, and helps build Fort Pulaski. His mother dies at Ravensworth, Fairfax County, Virginia.

1831   Lee is transferred to Fort Monroe, Virginia. He marries Mary Anna Randolph Custis at Arlington on June 30.

1834   Lee is transferred to Chief Engineer's Office in Washington.

1835   Lee resolves the Michigan-Ohio boundary as assistant to the Chief of Engineers.

1837   Lee is transferred to St. Louis to stabilize the harbor on the Mississippi River.

1838   Lee is promoted to captain.

1841   For five years, Lee supervises construction and repairs at Fort Hamilton and of the New York harbor fortifications.

1846   Serving for two years under Gen. John Wool and Gen. Winfield Scott in the Mexican War, Lee is breveted three times for bravery and daring reconnaissance.

1848   Lee supervises construction of Fort Carroll in Baltimore for nearly four years.

1852   Lee becomes superintendent of the U.S. Military Academy at West Point for three years. He strengthens the academic program and improves facilities.

1853   Lee's mother-in-law, Mary Custis, dies at Arlington.

1855   Lee is transferred from Engineers to Cavalry in Texas.

1857   Lee returns to manage Arlington estate when his father-in-law, G.W.P. Custis, dies.

1859

Lee commands federal troops at Harpers Ferry in capture of abolitionist John Brown.

1860

Lee returns to his Texas Regiment.

1861

Lee is ordered to Washington when Texas secedes. He accepts colonel's commission. He declines command of a Union Army. He resigns U.S. Army commission and accepts command of Virginia's military forces. After Virginia joins Confederacy, Lee serves as military adviser to President Jefferson Davis and leads troops in western Virginia.

1862

Lee is given command of the Army of Northern Virginia and successfully defends Richmond in Seven Days' Battle. He drives Union troops toward Washington and is victorious at Second Battle of Manassas. Lee's forces carry the war into Maryland and are driven back at Antietam. At Fredericksburg, Lee leads his 75,000-man force to victory over 113,000 Union soldiers.

1863

At Chancellorsville, Lee's men, outnumbered 2 to 1, defeat federal troops. Lee is decisively defeated at Gettysburg.

1864

Gen. Ulysses Grant begins a 10-month siege of Petersburg, cutting Lee's supply lines from the south.

1865

Lee is named general-in-chief of the Armies of the Confederacy. On April 2, with troops reduced to fewer than 30,000, he is forced to retreat from Petersburg and abandon Richmond. On April 9, Lee surrenders the Army of Northern Virginia to Grant at Appomattox Court House and returns to family in Richmond. In August he accepts presidency of Washington College in Lexington, Virginia.

1870

Robert E. Lee dies at Lexington October 12 and is buried in the college chapel.

1873

Mary Custis Lee dies at Lexington on November 5.

Part 2

The Historical Legacy

The Child of Mount Vernon

"The Washington Family" by Edward Savage depicts George and Martha Washington with two of her grandchildren, George Washington Parke Custis and Eleanor Parke Custis, 1796.

George Washington Parke Custis, a crayon likeness by Charles Fèvret de Saint-Mémin, 1805.

In 1781 Martha Washington's son by her first marriage, John Parke Custis, died of camp fever while serving as an aide to Gen. George Washington at Yorktown. To ease the burden upon Custis' young widow, the Washingtons brought home to Mount Vernon the couple's two youngest of four children, the 6-month-old George Washington Parke Custis and his 2½-year-old sister Eleanor Parke Custis. Martha Washington doted on "Tub" and "Nelly," overjoyed that her grandchildren were in perfect health and good spirits.

Young Custis was greatly influenced growing up in the presence of George Washington. An indifferent student, Custis nonetheless absorbed a strong sense of history and ideals from his guardian and the constant stream of distinguished visitors to Mount Vernon. Formal studies must have paled next to the bustle and ceremonial flurry of daily life in the Washington household. The Marquis de Lafayette, who spent considerable time at Mount Vernon, once recalled how young Custis, clutching Washington's hand, would tag along as the general showed visitors about the estate. Between the ages of 8 and 16, Custis witnessed the Washington presidency in New York and Philadelphia. He attended many theatrical productions and musical performances with Washington in both cities, watched him lay the cornerstone for the Capitol, and heard countless discussions about his guardian's hopes and dreams for America and its economic independence from Europe. Life with Washington imbued the young man with a reverence for American history, a thirst for progress, ideals of the Revolution, and a strong and energetic intellect that would serve him all his days.

The Washington Treasury

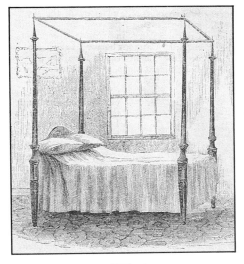

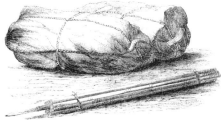

Washington's deathbed and war tents were among the treasured relics Benson J. Lossing illustrated in his article in "Harper's New Monthly Magazine" in 1853 after a visit to Arlington House.

The deaths of George and Martha Washington in 1799 and 1802 deeply affected Custis and closed a chapter in his life. Disappointed that he was unable to purchase Mount Vernon from Bushrod Washington, the general's nephew and heir, Custis prepared to leave Mount Vernon, taking with him his bequests from the Washingtons and as many relics and mementos as he was able to purchase from the estate.

Custis' portion of items from Martha Washington's estate included furniture, silver, china, and family portraits. At auctions in 1802 and 1803 Custis bought heavily; in the end he owed $4,545. His purchases included Washington's coach, tents used in the Revolution, and the Hessian and British flags presented Washington by Congress in honor of the final victory at Yorktown.

Custis decided to settle on his 1,100-acre tract overlooking the City of Washington that his father, John Custis, had purchased in 1778. He moved in 1802 to a four-room brick cottage at "Mount Washington"—a name later changed to Arlington after the Custis property on Virginia's Eastern Shore—with his precious store of Washington relics and began to plan a handsome house to hold the treasures from his boyhood home, Mount Vernon.

"A Very Showy Handsome Building"

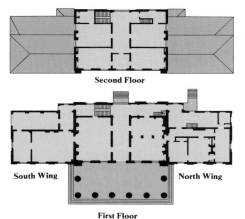

Second Floor

South Wing **North Wing**

First Floor

The Arlington House floor plan shows the north wing, which was completed in 1802, and the south wing, finished in 1804. The center of the mansion was not completed until 1818, when Custis' finances improved.

The earliest extant sketch of Arlington House was drawn by an unidentified artist in 1824.

Twenty-one-year-old G.W.P. Custis is believed to have engaged the professional services of George Hadfield, a young English architect, to draw plans for his house. Hadfield had studied in Italy and supervised part of the construction of the U.S. Capitol. The Greek Revival design of Arlington House features a two-story central section framed by an impressive Doric-columned portico and flanked north and south by lower wings. The site Custis selected for the mansion was a high bluff crowned with a forest of oak. The serene simplicity of the Arlington facade would be visible from the Capitol three miles away.

Undaunted by a shortage of funds to complete the project, Custis began work on the north wing in 1802 using materials from his estates. This wing was divided into living quarters and temporary space for the Washington treasury. The south wing was completed in 1804 and contained a large parlor and a smaller room that served as an office and study.

When Custis brought his young bride, Mary Lee "Molly" Fitzhugh, home to Arlington that year, they set up housekeeping in the north wing and entertained in the south wing. Even incomplete, the building was quite impressive. Cornelia Lee, a relative, wrote that during an 1804 visit Custis stopped caulking a boat long enough to offer a "glass of excellent wine" and a tour. "The House," she predicted, "will be a very showy handsome building when complete." After Robert E. Lee moved to Alexandria in 1811, he frequently visited Arlington and saw the house under construction.

The main section with its great portico was completed in 1818. By then Arlington House dominated the Virginia horizon opposite Washington.

14

Arlington House was first illustrated, above, in a tourist handbook, Washington Guide, *by William P. Elliott in 1826. Theseum, left, the Temple of Hephaestus in Athens, may have been architect George Hadfield's inspiration for the east portico and its pediment. The map, below, shows the extent of the Arlington estate about 1860. Arlington Spring is located south of the main house and near the canal.*

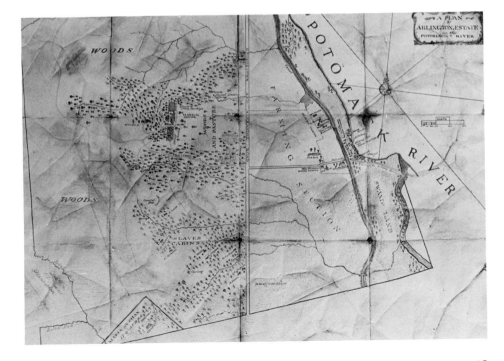

Artist, Dramatist, Scientific Farmer

G.W.P. Custis awarded this silver trophy to William H. Foote of Hayfield "In testimony of his having produced the Two finest Ewe Lambs of one year old at the Arlington Sheep Shearing in 1809." The cup was made by Alexandria silversmith Adam Lynn.

G.W.P. Custis possessed an intriguing combination of traits. He was a practical man, but he also was an idealist and an artist who found his highest calling in perpetuating the memory of George Washington through oratory, poems, heroic paintings, and preservation of his memorabilia.

Custis also was an unpretentious individual, as was his wife Molly. He liked to wear rough clothing and a battered hat about his farm. The farm activities he directed at Arlington were limited and experimental in character, and he relied on income from two farms on the Pamunkey River and land on Virginia's Eastern Shore to sustain the household.

The Custises had four children, but only their daughter, Mary Anna Randolph Custis, lived past the age of three. Custis left most of the child rearing to his wife and devoted his time to his many interests.

Custis was one of the first advocates of a U.S. Department of Agriculture. On his birthday in 1805 he inaugurated an annual sheep-shearing to encourage improved breeding and to help establish an independent American woolen industry. Those gatherings gave local farmers an opportunity to exhibit their best animals and homespun.

He wrote plays celebrating both heroic episodes in the nation's past and stirring current events. Produced from Boston to Charleston, they helped America create its own form of theater. Among his successes were "Pocahontas," commemorating the settling of Virginia, and "Railroad," an operetta praising technology and progress. His other writings included "Conversations with Lafayette," written after the aged general's visit to Arlington in 1825, and "Recollections and Private Memoirs of Washington."

Oil paintings by G.W.P. Custis commemorate the Revolutionary War battles (from left) of Trenton, Germantown, and Princeton. A self-trained artist, Custis recorded details of the battles related to him by Washington and other participants.

On April 11, 1836, Custis' play "Montgomerie, or the Orphans of a Wreck," set in 13th-century Scotland, opened at the National Theatre in Washington.

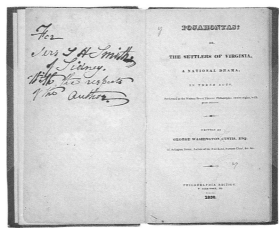

In 1830 Custis published "Pocahontas or the Settlers of Virginia," one of his "national dramas."

A Summer Wedding, 1831

Auguste Hervieu painted the oil portrait above of Mary Anna Randolph Custis shortly before her wedding. Lt. Robert E. Lee's portrait was done by William West in 1838.

"Never was I more surrounded with the joys of life than at this time," Mary Custis wrote to a friend in the fall of 1830. "I am engaged to one to whom I have been long attached—Robert Lee." The slim, dark-eyed daughter of George Washington Parke Custis and Molly Fitzhugh Custis had attracted many beaux, including the Tennessee frontiersman Sam Houston, but it was Lee, her distant cousin and childhood playmate, whose proposal she accepted.

Lee returned to his army post outside Savannah without a date set for the wedding. They were delighted the next spring with his transfer to Fort Monroe, Virginia, closer to Arlington. Plans for the wedding progressed. Lee wrote his brother Carter in New York to order wedding clothes: "I believe I will wear my uniform coat on the important night, & therefore *white* pantaloons must be in character.... Let the material of all be the best & *don't let* him charge too much."

Soon thereafter, Lee's commanding officer notified him he could take a one-month furlough, and a date was set for the wedding. Writing once again to Carter, Lee confided: "The day has been fixed & it is the 30th of June. I can tell you I begin to feel right *funny* when I count my days.... Can you come on to see it done?... I am told there are to be *six* pretty Bridesmaids, Misses Mason, Mary, Marietta, Angela, Julia and Brittannia & you could have some fine Kissing. For you know what a fellow you are at these weddings...."

Meanwhile a whirlwind of preparations was underway at Arlington, with extra quilts, mattresses, candlesticks, and silver being requisitioned from Aunt Maria Fitzhugh and others to supply the wedding party, close friends, and relations.

Rain fell steadily on the last day of June, but candlelight set the mansion aglow, reflecting the warm and happy atmosphere surrounding the festivities. The officiating clergyman, the Rev. Reuel Keith, arrived on horseback drenched to the skin. He was hastily fitted out in a coat and trousers belonging to the bride's father—too short and too wide by far for the rangy Mr. Keith, who managed to conceal his hilarious outfit beneath clerical robes.

Aunt Nelly Custis Lewis played music as Mary Custis entered the family parlor and took her place next to Lee, resplendent in his white trousers and dress uniform jacket, with its gold braid trim. The bride's hands trembled during the brief ceremony, Lee confided later to his commanding officer, and "The Parson had few words to say though he dwelt upon them as if he had been reading my Death warrant."

"This evening was one to be long remembered," Mary Lee's bridesmaid and cousin Marietta Turner recalled. "My cousin, always a modest and affectionate girl, was never lovelier, and Robert Lee with his bright eyes and high color was the picture of a cavalier. The elegance and simplicity of the bride's parents, presiding over the feast, and the happiness of the grinning servants . . . remain in my memory as a piece of Virginia life pleasant to recall."

Following the custom of the day, the couple remained at Arlington with the wedding party, gathering on the Fourth of July for a final round of festivities at the home of family friends on Analostan (now Roosevelt) Island. A few weeks later, Lt. and Mrs. Lee accompanied Mrs. Custis on a trip to visit relatives. At the end of the summer the Lees went to Fort Monroe, where he resumed his army duties.

The marriage vows exchanged at Arlington by Mary and Robert Lee in the summer of 1831 bridged the loneliness that was inevitable in a soldier's life and supported husband and wife as their family grew to include seven children, three sons and four daughters. The family usually traveled with Lee to his various posts, and Mrs. Lee returned to Arlington for the births of six of their seven children. The whole family customarily returned to Arlington in the winter when engineering projects closed down.

Lee respected his wife's parents as his own, mindful of Custis' warm reception of him as a son and Molly Custis' unfailing kindness to him throughout his boyhood. She was one of the few relatives in attendance when Robert's mother, Ann Carter Lee, died in 1829 at Ravensworth, the Fitzhugh estate.

The Lees were a study in contrasts: she, outspoken, casual in appearance and housekeeping, artistic and impulsive; and he, reserved, gracious and whimsical, punctual, thrifty, and a born organizer. They were devoted parents anxious that each of their children learn their responsibilities and fulfill their duties. Their mutual affection was constant and a source of strength through many separations and the final loss of their beloved Arlington.

Writing to Mary on June 30, 1864, under Union fire in the trenches of Petersburg, Lee asked, "Do you recollect what a happy day thirty-three years ago this was? How many hopes and pleasures it gave birth to!"

Both the Custis and Lee families immigrated to Virginia from England in the 1600s and acquired large landholdings. In 1750 Daniel Parke Custis wed Martha Dandridge, and after his death seven years later his widow took over the man-agement of extensive lands, fisheries, gristmills, and other businesses. In 1759 Martha Custis married a young officer, Col. George Washington, and moved with her two children, John Parke, 4, and Martha, 2, to Mount Vernon. Her son, known as Jackie, married Eleanor Calvert, a granddaughter of the sixth Lord Baltimore, in 1774. After his death in 1781, the two youngest of John Custis' four children, George Washington Parke Custis and Nelly, were raised by General and Mrs. Washington as their

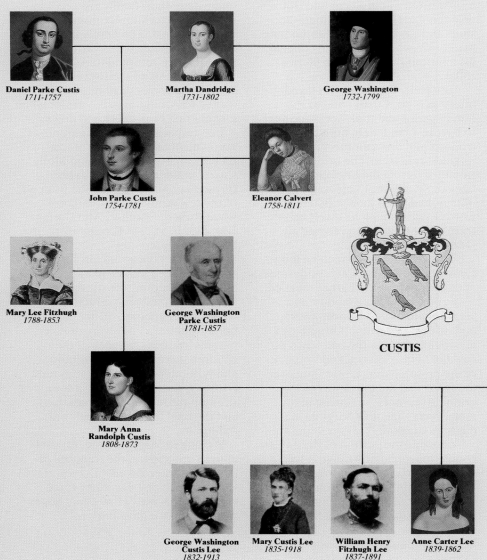

Daniel Parke Custis
1711-1757

Martha Dandridge
1731-1802

George Washington
1732-1799

John Parke Custis
1754-1781

Eleanor Calvert
1758-1811

Mary Lee Fitzhugh
1788-1853

George Washington Parke Custis
1781-1857

CUSTIS

Mary Anna Randolph Custis
1808-1873

George Washington Custis Lee
1832-1913

Mary Custis Lee
1835-1918

William Henry Fitzhugh Lee
1837-1891

Anne Carter Lee
1839-1862

own children at Mount Vernon. In 1804, G.W.P. Custis married Mary Lee "Molly" Fitzhugh, and in 1808 they had a daughter, Mary Anna Randolph Custis. This great-granddaughter of Martha Washington grew up at Arlington and there mar- ried Robert E. Lee in 1831. A sixth-generation Virginian, Lee counted among his forebears judges, military officers, and legislators. Two of his father's cousins signed the Declaration of Independence. Born at Stratford Hall in 1807, Robert was the fifth child of Ann Hill Carter and Henry "Light Horse Harry" Lee. His mother had been raised at Shirley, the Carter family plantation on the James River. His father was known as a Revolutionary hero, governor of Virginia, and member of Congress.

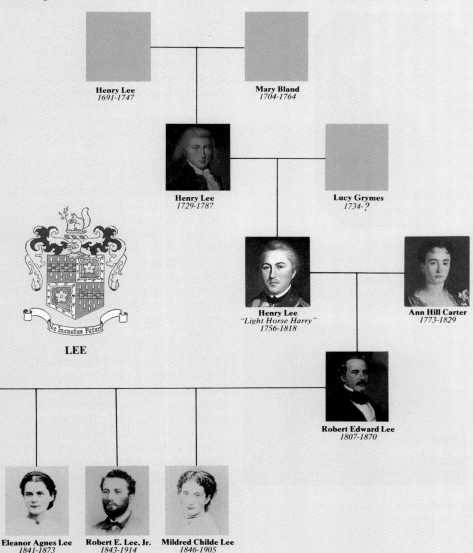

Henry Lee
1691-1747

Mary Bland
1704-1764

Henry Lee
1729-1787

Lucy Grymes
1734-?

LEE

Henry Lee
"Light Horse Harry"
1756-1818

Ann Hill Carter
1773-1829

Robert Edward Lee
1807-1870

Eleanor Agnes Lee
1841-1873

Robert E. Lee, Jr.
1843-1914

Mildred Childe Lee
1846-1905

Christmas Puddings and Summer Picnics

Robert E. Lee and his son William Henry Fitzhugh are dressed for the holidays in this photograph taken in 1845, when William, known as "Rooney," was 8.

This oil painting of Arlington Spring shows the dance hall and dining pavilion in 1859.

In the transitory life of a military family, Arlington House represented permanency, and Christmas at the beloved homestead was a particularly happy season of reunion. The Lees were together at Arlington for 24 of the 30 Christmas seasons they celebrated before the Civil War. In 1846, one of the Christmases he missed, Lee wrote to sons Custis and Rooney: "I hope good Santa Claus will fill my Rob's stocking to-night: that Mildred's, Agnes's, and Anna's may break down with good things. I do not know what he may have for you and Mary, but if he only leaves for you one half of what I wish, you will want for nothing!"

For son Custis at West Point in 1851, Lee summed up the family's holiday visit to the Custises at Arlington: "The children were delighted at getting back, and passed the evening in devising pleasure for the morrow. They were in upon us before day on Christmas to overhaul their stockings . . . I need not describe to you our amusements, you have witnessed them so often; nor the turkey, cold ham, plum pudding, mince pies, etc., at dinner."

The hospitality of Arlington spread far beyond the family circle. G.W.P. Custis opened Arlington Spring on the Potomac to picnicking parties from Georgetown, Washington, and Alexandria. Custis added a dancing pavilion and kitchen, and he loved to mingle with visitors, playing his violin, singing songs of the Revolution, and telling anecdotes and jokes.

*Benson J. Lossing made this
watercolor sketch of Arlington
House in 1853.*

Slavery at Arlington House

The Custis family had held slaves since the 17th century. George Washington Parke Custis sought a solution to the problem of slavery and became an active member of the American Colonization Society, organized to help freed slaves return to west Africa. At its 1826 annual meeting, Custis called slavery "the mightiest serpent that ever infested the world," declaring that 200 years of slavery in the South had not accomplished as much as one generation of free men in the West. When he died in 1857, Custis owned more than 60 slaves at Arlington and more than that at his Pamunkey River farms near Williamsburg. Custis' will provided that his slaves be freed at his death if the estate were free of debt. It included a stipulation that if there were

The slaves of the Arlington household include Sally and Leonard Norris, top, and their daughter, Selina Gray.

Simple furniture such as this table, used in the main house or in the servants' quarters, was made by slaves at Arlington.

24

debts they could be held up to five years. Custis and especially Lee had become targets of the abolitionist press. The December 30, 1857, *New York Times* reported that Custis had made a deathbed pledge to his slaves that they would be freed in his will, and that the will was now being kept secret. Lee, as executor of the Custis estate, wrote to the *Times* to refute the story, observing that the will had been submitted for probate before the Alexandria County Court and was open for public inspection. Since the estate was seriously in debt, Lee held the slaves until 1862, when he freed them. From the battlefield, he wrote his son, G.W. Custis Lee, "They are entitled to their freedom and I wish to give it to them."

A member of the Lee family sketched the north servants' quarters, above, about 1855-57. The sketch was found in an old family scrapbook. Robert E. Lee, executor of the G.W.P. Custis estate, certified the inventory, left, of slaves at Arlington in 1858.

United States Army Officer

Mementos of an Army life: Lee's U.S. Army Corps of Engineers insignia, his Confederate mess kit, and his traveling chess set.

Robert E. Lee began his impressive military career as a lieutenant in the Corps of Engineers, and his first assignment was to work on the construction of Fort Pulaski near Savannah. Transferred to Fort Monroe, Virginia, in 1831, he continued his work on harbor defenses. He then was posted to Washington as assistant to the Chief of Engineers in 1834 and on a temporary assignment to survey and resolve the Michigan-Ohio boundary in 1835. He was assigned in 1837 to St. Louis to work on stabilizing the Mississippi River channel and was promoted to captain in 1838. His success at St. Louis established his reputation as an engineer, and he was assigned to Fort Hamilton in 1841 to work on the New York harbor fortifications.

When war with Mexico broke out in 1846, Lee welcomed combat service and spent two years in Mexico as an engineering officer in reconnaissance and staff operations. Lee was praised for his "gallantry and good conduct," for construction of fortifications, and for performance under "the heavy fire of the enemy." Gen. Winfield Scott called him "the very best soldier that I ever saw in the field."

The war gave him experience in planning strategy and handling troops. Promoted to the brevet ranks of major, lieutenant colonel, and colonel for gallantry and meritorious service, Lee returned from Mexico to a happy reunion with his loved ones. Assigned to Baltimore in 1848, he supervised construction of Fort Carroll for nearly four years.

The U.S. Military Academy at West Point, New York, became home to the Lees in 1852, when Lee was appointed superintendent. G. W. Custis Lee graduated first in his class there in

1854. And Lee, in his three-year tenure, raised academic standards, lengthened the program from four to five years, and improved facilities.

In 1855 Lee was transferred from the Engineers to the 2nd U.S. Cavalry regiment being organized for duty on the Texas frontier. Mary and the family returned to Arlington, where she helped her elderly father manage the estate. In October 1857 Custis died, and Lee returned to Arlington, requesting a leave of absence to administer the estate as the only qualifying executor. In 1859, while still at Arlington, Lee was given command of federal forces sent to capture the abolitionist John Brown at Harpers Ferry.

Lee left Arlington in early 1860 to rejoin his regiment in Texas and uneasily watched his country slip toward civil war. On January 22, 1861, he wrote to Markie Williams: "I am unable to realize that our people will destroy a government inaugurated in the blood and wisdom of our patriot fathers, that has given us peace and prosperity at home, power and security abroad, and under which we have acquired colossal strength unequalled in the history of mankind. I wish to live under no other government and there is no sacrifice I am not ready to make for the preservation of the Union, save that of honour."

On the next day, Lee wrote to his son Custis: "If the Union is dissolved, and the Government disrupted, I shall return to my native State and share the miseries of my people, and save in defence will draw my sword on none." On February 1 Texas seceded from the Union and Lee was ordered back to Washington. He arrived on March 1 and was promoted to colonel of the 1st Cavalry on March 16. Abraham Lincoln signed the commission on March 28.

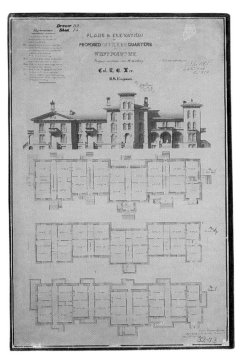

These new quarters for married and single officers were built at West Point during Colonel Lee's term as superintendent.

Lee's Fateful Decision

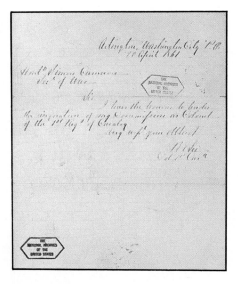

Col. Robert E. Lee's April 20, 1861, letter of resignation from the U.S. Army is located at the National Archives in Washington.

At 4:30 a.m. on April 12, 1861, South Carolina shore batteries opened fire on Fort Sumter in Charleston harbor. The federal forces surrendered on April 14 without casualties, but the attack by a secessionist state forced the Union to action. On April 15 President Lincoln declared the existence of an "insurrection" and called for 75,000 volunteers to give three months of military service. By that time seven states had left the Union, but not Virginia.

The war Lee had long dreaded was at hand. For the North, with a population of 22 million, a strong and balanced economy, a well-developed railroad grid, and naval supremacy, the war began as one to restore the Union, though slavery was an underlying issue. The 11 states that eventually formed the Confederacy had 9 million inhabitants (including 3.5 million slaves), an agricultural economy, and inadequate railroad systems. Overall the Confederacy appeared woefully weak as it declared its independence.

Lee still awaited Virginia's decision. Unbeknownst to him, the Virginia Secession Convention in a secret session on April 17 passed the Ordinance of Secession 88 to 55. On April 18 Lee met with Francis P. Blair, Sr., at his home across from the White House. Blair, acting on behalf of President Lincoln, offered Lee command of the army being raised to fight the Confederacy. Lee declined. After the war he recalled telling Blair "as candidly and courteously as I could, that though opposed to secession and deprecating war, I could take no part in an invasion of the Southern states." Lee left Blair's home and met with Gen. Winfield Scott in the War Department across the street and told his old friend what had transpired.

Not until April 19 did Lee learn that the Virginia Convention had adopted the Ordinance of Secession to be confirmed by public referendum on May 23. Lee knew he must act quickly if he wished to resign before receiving orders. As anxious friends and relatives gathered at Arlington House to discuss the deteriorating situation, Lee walked alone in the garden. He later went to his bed chamber—pacing the floor and pausing to kneel in prayer. Shortly after midnight, he emerged with his letter of resignation.

Lee's decision cost him his Union Army career and Arlington House, and it separated him from friends and relatives who would remain with the Union. To his brother, Sydney Smith Lee, he wrote: "I wished to wait till the Ordinance of Secession should be acted on by the people of Virginia; but war seems to have commenced, and I am liable at any time to be ordered on duty, which I could not conscientiously perform. To save me from such a position and to prevent the necessity of resigning under orders, I had to act at once. . . ."

On April 21, the governor of Virginia asked Lee to take command of the state's military forces, an offer he felt he could not refuse. The next day he left for Richmond to accept the command. He was never to return to Arlington.

For four years Lee's audacity, brilliance, and charismatic leadership inspired the Army of Northern Virginia and the South. But the North's overwhelming advantages in troops and supplies ultimately prevailed, and Gen. Ulysses S. Grant finally took Richmond, the Confederate Capital, on April 3, 1865. On April 9, Gen. Robert E. Lee surrendered to Grant at Appomattox Court House.

In this 1864 photograph, Robert E. Lee wears his full dress Confederate general's uniform with military sash and dress sword. The photograph was taken in Richmond by Julian Vannerson as part of a series that was sent to the Berlin studio of a Virginian, Edward V. Valentine, to use in making a statue of Lee.

Robert E. Lee left Arlington House on April 22, 1861. Mrs. Lee remained behind and began packing family possessions and moving them to places of safety. Her husband and family members almost daily urged her to leave, but she stayed until her son Custis resigned his army commission about May 15. Federal troops crossed the Potomac and occupied northern Virginia and the Arlington estate on May 24. For the four years of the Civil War Arlington was an armed camp. Gen. George McClellan and others used the house as an army headquarters and drilled units of the Army of the Potomac here. The ancient forests of oaks, elms, and chestnuts were leveled to build fortifications and barracks and to supply firewood. Visiting Ar-

Four views of Arlington House during its occupation by Union forces show troops standing at attention on the south side of the portico and at ease on the front steps. At left above is Maj. Irvin McDowell and his staff in 1861; just below, Gen.

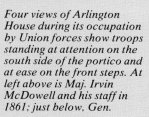

Samuel Peter Heintzelmann stands with officers of the 71st infantry in 1862.

lington in July 1862, cousin Markie Williams noted the "poor House looked so desolate" and "strangely distorted." The scenes she had known so well as a member of the household were now offices and quarters for Union soldiers. In the early years of the war, sympathetic Union officers, especially those who had served with Lee in the U.S. Army, attempted to preserve the house and grounds. But these constraints yielded to wartime conditions; trenches, rifle pits, and earthwork forts were built for the defense of Washington, and military roads soon crisscrossed the fields and hillsides of Arlington. By 1863 many Union leaders considered Lee a traitor and wanted to make an example of his home as a warning to others.

The Union Army pressed into service the G.W.P. Custis, an excursion boat that ran between Washington and Arlington Spring, and with a balloon from a new deck conducted aerial reconnaissance of Confederate operations on the Potomac.

On May 13, 1864, William Christman of Pennsylvania became the first Union soldier buried at Arlington. After the estate was seized, Maj. Gen. M.C. Meigs selected 200 acres surrounding the house as a national cemetery for the Union dead.

For the March 7, 1864, issue of "Harper's Weekly," A.R. Waud sketched this view of Freedman's Village, established at Arlington in 1863 as a community for about 2,000 emancipated slaves.

Part 3

The House and Grounds

Visiting the Estate

The front door knocker was taken as a souvenir of Arlington by a Union soldier and later returned.

Family portraits cover the walls of the entrance hall. They include (center) a copy of Charles Willson Peale's portrait of George Washington, made by Ernest Fischer for Colonel and Mrs. Lee and carried with them to military quarters after 1850. Above it is a painting Fischer copied from a John Wollaston portrait of Martha Washington, and (left) a copy of the equestrian portrait of Washington at Yorktown by G.W.P. Custis.

Pages 32-33: The White Parlor, shown decked with holiday greenery, was completed by Colonel and Mrs. Lee in 1855 and furnished with crimson upholstered furniture they brought with them from West Point. The marble mantels in the room were designed for Lee in New York City.

Alighting from carriages before the great columned portico of Arlington, guests in the 19th century were surely as moved as today's visitor by the breathtaking panorama of the Nation's Capital spread before them.

For more than 50 years Arlington House was first and foremost a home to a lively brood of Custises and Lees, an extended family that included George and Molly Custis, Robert E. and Mary Custis Lee, and the Lees' four daughters and three sons. The tall Greek Revival front doors of Arlington, open during all but the coldest months of the year, welcomed waves of aunts, uncles, cousins, friends, and even strangers drawn to the mansion by its legacy of Washington relics and memories. The Arlington atmosphere exemplified Virginia hospitality; expected or not, guests were made to feel at home and often urged to linger for a longer visit.

In the same spirit the National Park Service today invites you to visit Arlington House and immerse yourself in its history as a family estate. The house and its furnishings provide tangible links with early America. As you take the self-guiding tour, imagine the family gatherings and daily routines that took place here. Also, walk about the grounds and visit the outbuildings, museum, and bookstore.

The house is open daily; the hours vary seasonally. Subway service from Washington and Alexandria is available on Blue Line trains. You may park your car at the Arlington Cemetery Visitor Center and walk, or ride the bus service, to the house.

For more information, ask the staff at the house or write to: Superintendent, George Washington Memorial Parkway, Turkey Run Park, McLean, VA 22102.

34

Family Parlor and Dining Room

The first room to the right off the entrance hall, the family parlor, was the center of daily life for the Lees and Custises. Each day began in the parlor with morning prayers attended by the entire household—family members, servants, and guests. When President Pierce's wife visited the house she found the parlor to be "a preeminently social room." Another visitor concurred in 1856: "I like this room; it is not the least bit in order." A Custis cousin, Elizabeth Randolph Calvert, described the room's furniture in her 1840s visit: "On either side of the fireplaces . . . are two chairs, large and square. . . . The one to the right with its back to the window is exclusively the seat of Mr. Custis and his cat, a yellow brindled cat." It was in this room that

Hanging on the north wall of the family parlor is the original portrait, center, of Mary Anna Randolph Custis by Auguste Hervieu in 1831 just before her marriage to Robert E. Lee. The green silk-covered furniture was acquired by the Custises about 1825. The traveling desk, right, belonged to Lee, a constant correspondent with his family.

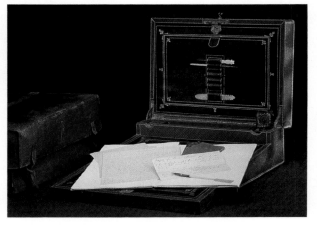

36

Mary Custis and Robert E. Lee were married in 1831. And each Christmas the Yule log was kindled on the family parlor hearth with a piece of the previous year's log. After morning devotions, breakfast was served in the adjoining family dining room. It was Lee's custom to gather rosebuds each morning and place one on the plate of each lady. The dining room table, customarily resting on a crumb cloth covering the floor, was set with family china and silver. Sometimes each place was set with everyday blue and white Canton china framed by silver of the fiddle thread pattern engraved with the Lee crest, a squirrel. Here half a dozen future Confederate and Union generals celebrated Washington's Birthday at a dinner party in 1861.

Family furnishings in the dining room and parlor include Mount Vernon knife boxes, an American tea kitchen engraved with the Lee coat of arms, and an 18th-century Canton bowl inherited by the Custis and Lee families.

"I have an excellent studio fitted up in the South Wing of the House, with a first-rate light," G.W.P. Custis wrote in 1852. In his sunny studio Custis painted his Revolutionary War pictures of George Washington, his favorite theme. After Custis' death, Mary Custis Lee used the adjoining room to attend to estate business. Here, in her morning room, she edited her father's memoirs and pursued her painting. Arthritis limited her movements and kept her in this room most of each day.

Furnishings in the office, above, include the desk used by Lee in Baltimore and restored to Arlington in 1913.

In the south end of the morning room is Custis' 8-by-12-foot "Battle of Monmouth," right, which was painted for a niche in the U.S. Capitol and returned when John Trumball's paintings arrived. It was taken to Tudor Place in Georgetown by Markie Williams during the Civil War and returned by her relatives in the 1970s.

Above the parlors and dining room of the first floor are the bed chambers of the Lees and their seven children. Each chamber opens onto the upper hall, used in summer as a sitting room to catch cooling breezes. Carpets covered the random width pine floors in winter, and grass matting was used in summer. Colonel and Mrs. Lee's chamber, located in the southwest corner, overlooks the flower garden. It was to this room above the White Parlor that Lee retired the night of April 19, 1861, to write his letter of resignation from the U.S. Army. On April 22 he packed and left Arlington to answer the call of his native state. Mrs. Lee followed him south within a month. A musket and powder horns above the fireplace identify the next room on the

The Lees' bed chamber contains a family bed. Personal effects of Mary Lee include her English silver card case and a pair of monogrammed glass perfume decanters.

south side as the Lee boys' chamber. It was shared by Custis, Rooney, and Robert Lee, Jr. Mary Lee had her own bedroom at the northeast corner of the house overlooking the city. She shared it with cousin Markie Williams in the 1850s. On the east side of the house, between Mary's room and the boys' room, is a small chamber that was used by guests. Mrs. Lee created this room by combining two dressing rooms and having a doorway cut into the upper hall. Across the hall from their parents' room is the bed chamber of Agnes, Annie, and Mildred Lee. The Washington bed from Mount Vernon was in this room. Next to that is a dressing room used as a playroom. Here Annie Lee conducted Sunday School for the children of family servants.

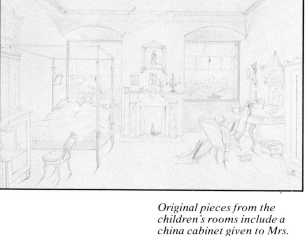

Original pieces from the children's rooms include a china cabinet given to Mrs. Lee when she was a young girl and a statue, "Three Graces," a gift from George Custis to his granddaughters. "Roughing it at Arlington" is the humorous title given by the artist, a Union soldier, to this sketch of the Lee girls' bed chamber showing the statue in place on the mantel and shades in the windows.

The first section of Arlington House to be built, the north wing, served as living quarters for George and Molly Custis during the early years of the mansion's construction. Later these chambers became guest quarters, but as the Lee family grew, the Custises reoccupied their original suite off the family parlor, and in the 1850s Lee had the mansion's first bathroom with modern fixtures installed near these rooms. A small room at the north end of the house was used for sewing and for classes for the children. Fireplaces and stoves heated the north wing. Below the main floor is the winter kitchen, where servants cooked the family's food and washed the laundry. Glassware and serving dishes were stored in large cupboards, and stoneware crocks

The pine cabinet, a gift from Mrs. Lee to a family servant, Selina Gray, was returned by a Gray descendant to the mansion.

Servants prepared meals for the Custis and Lee families in the winter kitchen using fresh vegetables and fruits of the season.

held cider made from apples grown locally. Apple brandy and blackberry wine were among commodities produced at Arlington. The grapes and berries were grown with vegetables in the garden north of the mansion. A stock of domestic and foreign wines was kept in the wine cellar. The dairy was located in the south wing. Here, for you to try, is Mrs. Lee's recipe for gingerbread cookies, a favorite of the Christmas season:

3 lbs. flour *(12 cups)*
1 lb. butter *(2 cups)*
1 lb. sugar *(2 cups)*
1 oz. ginger *(one-eighth cup)*
1 lb. molasses *(2 cups)*
¼ pt. cream *(½ cup)*
Roll thin to a uniform thickness; cut with small glass or cookie cutter; bake at 375° about 6 minutes, or until done.

Gardens to the south and north of Arlington House provided flowers and vegetables to the household during much of the year. The south flower garden, laid out by George Custis with the help of a former Mount Vernon gardener, was a favorite di-version of Molly Custis, her daughter Mary Lee—both gifted gardeners—and granddaughters. Gravel paths radiated from a central arbor, whose wood frame was covered with yellow jasmine and honeysuckle. Several species of fragrant roses were cultivated here. Among Mrs. Custis' favorite flowers were hearteases and lilies-of-the-valley. Robert E. Lee loved to visit the garden on spring and summer mornings, inspecting the roses and gathering buds for the breakfast table. A kitchen garden off

The flower garden at Arlington served not only as an outlet for Molly Custis and Mary Lee's interest in rose cultivation, but as a favorite gathering place and retreat for all members of the family. Each Lee daughter was given her own small plot on which to raise whatever flowers she pleased, and generations of household pets were laid to rest along its paths. The Lee daughters remembered taking novels to the arbor to read, for their father thought they should read only non-fiction.

the north wing included strawberry and asparagus beds, cherry, plum, pear and apricot trees, raspberries, gooseberries, peas, beans, potatoes, rhubarb, leeks, corn, and more—on less than an acre! The two low buildings on the west side of the mansion provided living quarters for household servants and formed a rear courtyard with the mansion. The south building was known as "Selina's House," for its west end was occupied by Mrs. Lee's personal maid and housekeeper, Selina Gray, and her family. The middle room was used for storing meat, and a storeroom at the east end held other household provisions. The corresponding north building housed other servants, and its cellar served as a summer kitchen.

The small panels above the doors of the south servants' quarters were decorated by George Custis with paintings of American eagles and George Washington's war horse. As these details of the servants' quarters indicate, the two buildings were designed to harmonize with the mansion and carry out the Greek theme with small arches and pillars.

"Uncle Joe," a name given an elderly servant at Arlington by Union soldiers, sits in the doorway of the north servants' quarters, top.

1 Mount Vernon, Mount Vernon, Virginia 22121. Located on the Potomac 17 miles south of Arlington, Mount Vernon was George Washington's home for 45 years. Here George Washington Parke Custis and his sister Nelly were raised by the Washingtons after the death of their father, Martha Washington's son John Custis. The property, owned since 1858 by the Mount Vernon Ladies' Association of the Union, is open every day of the year from 9 to 4 p.m. November to March and 9 a.m. to 5 p.m. March to November.

2 Shirley Plantation, Rt. 5, Charles City, Virginia 23030. Since its founding in 1613, Shirley has been a working plantation owned by the Hill-Carter family. Shirley was the home and wedding place of Ann Hill Carter, Robert E. Lee's mother. Lee visited Shirley many times, and his son Rooney married Charlotte Wickham here in 1859. This National Historic Landmark is 135 miles south of Washington.

3 Stratford Hall, Stratford, Virginia 22558. Robert E. Lee was born here January 19, 1807. The house was built in the 1720s by Thomas Lee, a planter and acting governor of Virginia and father of two signers of the Declaration of Independence. For a century Stratford was the home of this distinguished family. Throughout his life Lee remembered it with affection. The Stratford museum contains Robert E. Lee memorabilia.

Robert E. Lee Boyhood Home, 607 Oronoco Street, Alexandria, Virginia, 22314. This Fitzhugh family townhouse was the site of the wedding of Mary Lee Fitzhugh to George Custis in 1804. This was Lee's home from 1812 to 1816 and 1820 to 1825, when he went to West Point.

The United States Military Academy, West Point, New York 10996. From 1852 to 1855 Robert E. Lee, an 1829 graduate, was superintendent. In the museum is Lee's Appomattox sash.

4 Fort Pulaski National Monument, P.O. Box 98, Tybee Island, Georgia 31328. This was Lee's first army posting after graduating from West Point in 1829.

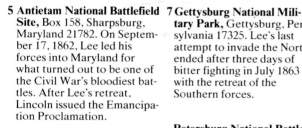

5 Antietam National Battlefield Site, Box 158, Sharpsburg, Maryland 21782. On September 17, 1862, Lee led his forces into Maryland for what turned out to be one of the Civil War's bloodiest battles. After Lee's retreat, Lincoln issued the Emancipation Proclamation.

6 Fredericksburg and Spotsylvania County Battlefields Memorial National Military Park, P.O. Box 679, Fredericksburg, Virginia 22401. The battles of Fredericksburg and Chancellorsville ended in Confederate victories. Those of Wilderness and Spotsylvania Court House were indecisive. Chatham Manor, the Fitzhugh family home and birthplace of Mary Lee Fitzhugh Custis in 1788, is in the park.

7 Gettysburg National Military Park, Gettysburg, Pennsylvania 17325. Lee's last attempt to invade the North ended after three days of bitter fighting in July 1863 with the retreat of the Southern forces.

Petersburg National Battlefield, P.O. Box 549, Petersburg, Virginia 23803. The fall of Petersburg April 2, 1865, after a 10-month siege signaled the beginning of the end of the Civil War.

Richmond National Battlefield Park, 3215 E. Broad, Richmond, Virginia 23223. This park in the former capital of the Confederacy commemorates the Seven Days' Battles, Cold Harbor, and other Civil War battles.

8 Appomattox Court House National Historical Park, Appomattox, Virginia 24522. Here Robert E. Lee surrendered the Army of Northern Virginia to Ulysses S. Grant on April 9, 1865. Lee memorabilia is on display.

9 Lee Chapel and Museum, Washington and Lee University, Lexington, Virginia 24450. Built at Robert E. Lee's request in 1866, the Lee Chapel is the final resting place of General Lee, his wife, mother, father, and all but one of his children. His beloved horse Traveller is buried nearby. Family possessions, including many original Arlington portraits, are displayed in the museum. The college president's house was planned, built, and used by Lee.

National Park Service

The National Park Service expresses its appreciation to all those persons who made the preparation and production of this handbook possible. The Service especially thanks the Parks and History Association for its financial support of this publication and the Lee family for making Lee memorabilia available.

The creative development of this handbook was done by Staples & Charles Ltd. of Washington, D.C. The text was written by Nancy Growald Brooks based upon National Park Service research by Murray H. Nelligan and information provided by Agnes Mullins, curator of Arlington House. Other sources include *Recollections and Letters of General Robert E. Lee,* by Robert E. Lee, Jr., Doubleday, Page & Company, 1924, and *R.E. Lee. A Biography,* by Douglas Southall Freeman, Vol. I, Charles Scribner's Sons, 1934.

Unless credited below, the illustrations come from the files of Arlington House and the National Park Service or from the Lee family: Dietrich Brothers, American Corp. 17 paintings; Dorchester Historical Society 24 Norrises; Robert E. Lee Memorial Association 46 Stratford; Library of Congress 15 Elliott, 17 "Pocahontas," 30-31 Freedman's Village; Maxwell MacKenzie cover, 4-5, 10-11; Mount Vernon 20 G.W.P. Custis, 46 Mount Vernon; National Air and Space Museum, 31 balloon; National Archives 27, 28 by David R. Allison, 30 Civil War photos; National Gallery of Art 12 Washington family; Shirley Plantation 46 Shirley; Staples & Charles 6, 8 revolver, 13, 16, 17 broadside, 24 table, 26, 31 grave, 32-45; U.S. Military Academy, West Point 21 R.E. Lee; Valentine Museum 9 Traveller, 29; Virginia Historical Society 14 earliest sketch, 21 Henry Lee 1729, 22 Lee and Rooney; Virginia Museum of Fine Arts 20 J.P. Custis; Washington and Lee University 8 Mary Custis, 18 Lee, 47 Lee Chapel; White House 20 Washington and Dandridge. The Service thanks Mrs. A. Smith Bowman for the picture of G.W.P. Custis on page 12 and Mrs. J. William Rose for Eleanor Calvert, 20.